WHO'S A FRIEND OF THE WATER-SPURTING

WHALE

BY

SANNA ANDERSON BAKER

HANDLETTERED AND ILLUSTRATED BY

TOMIE dePAOLA

Chariot Books
DAVID C. COOK PUBLISHING CO.

FOR GABRIELLE
S.A.B.

FOR KATHY AND BOB CHANDLER
T. deP.

Chariot Books is an imprint of David C. Cook Publishing Co.

David C. Cook Publishing Co., Elgin, Illinois 60120
David C. Cook Publishing Co., Weston, Ontario

WHO'S A FRIEND OF THE WATER-SPURTING WHALE?

First Printing, 1987

Printed in Singapore

91 90 89 88   2 3 4 5

Library of Congress Cataloging-in-Publication Data

Baker, Sanna Anderson.
Who's a friend of the water-spurting whale?

Summary: Tells in rhyme of God's control of the elements
and His loving care of Earth's animals.
1. Providence and government of God—Juvenile literature.
[1. God] I. dePaola, Tomie, ill. II. Title.
BT96.2.B33   1986   231'.5   85-28084
ISBN 0-89191-587-7

WHO KNOWS

THE WAY
TO THE HOUSE OF LIGHT ?
AND WHO KNOWS
WHERE
DARKNESS DWELLS ?

WHO WAS THERE
WHEN
THE SEA WAS BORN ?
AND
WHO WRAPS IT ROUND
WITH
A BLANKET OF FOG ?

GOD

WHO
TELLS MORNING,
"SWEEP THE STARS FROM THE SKY"?

AND
WHO SHAPES THE CLOUDS
THAT HANG SO HIGH?

WHO SAYS TO THUNDER,
"WHEN LIGHTNING DANCES,
CLAP"?

WHO SAYS TO SNOW,
"GO TO EARTH,
AND
BE QUIET
AS A CAT"?

WHO TELLS THE STORM
TO ROAR
LIKE A LION?
AND
WHO MAKES LAKES
FREEZE
HARD AS IRON?

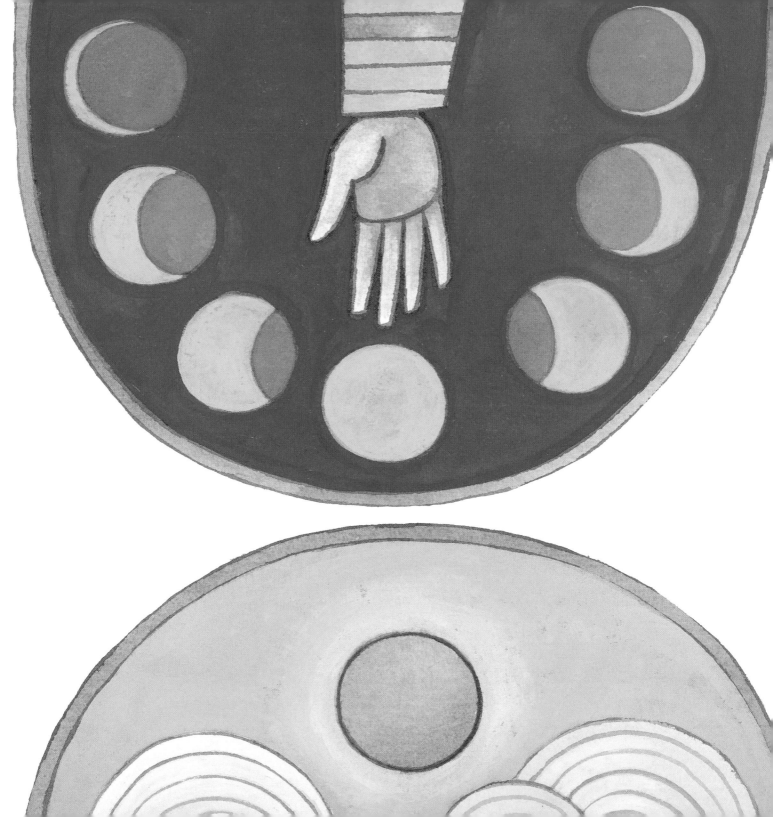

GOD

WHO'S A FRIEND
OF THE BEASTS
IN THE FOREST?

WHO
TAKES CARE
OF THE CATTLE?

WHO FINDS FOOD
FOR THE LION AND HER YOUNG?

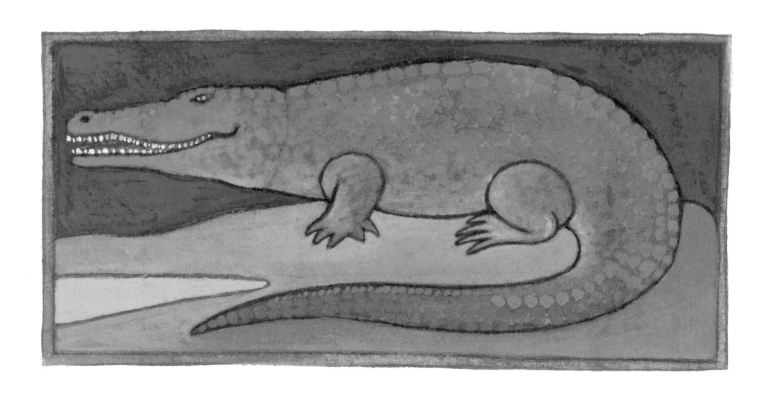

WHO
MADE THE CROCODILE'S JAWS
SO STRONG?

WHO KNOWS THE NAMES
OF THE BIRDS
OF THE WORLD?

AND
WHO'S A FRIEND
OF THE WATER-SPURTING WHALE?

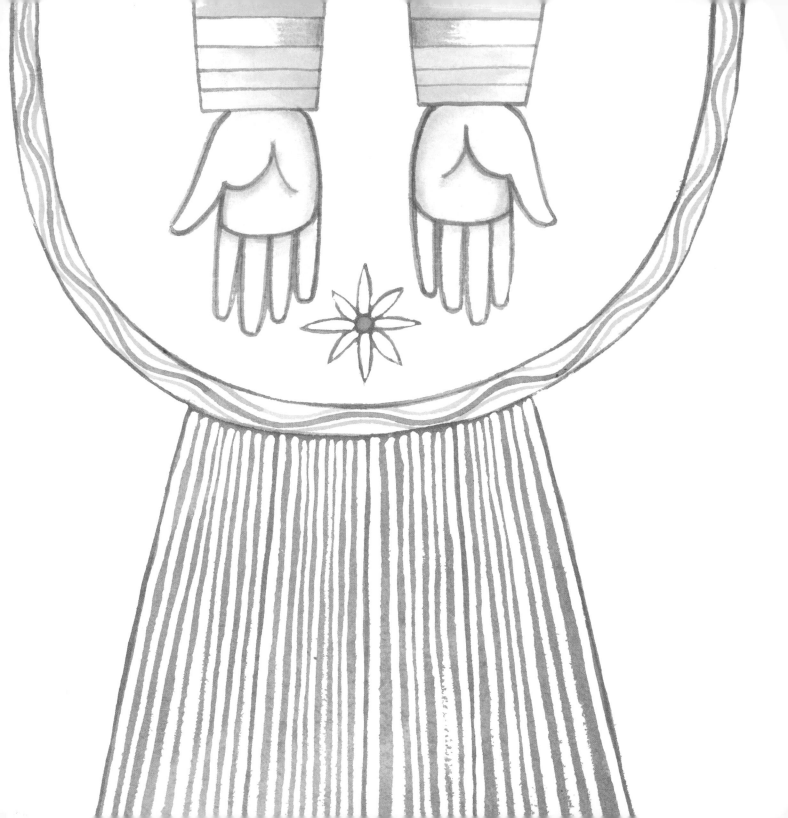

GOD

HE IS GREAT.

AND HE IS GOOD.

BASED ON PASSAGES
FROM THE OLD TESTAMENT
THE BOOK OF JOB